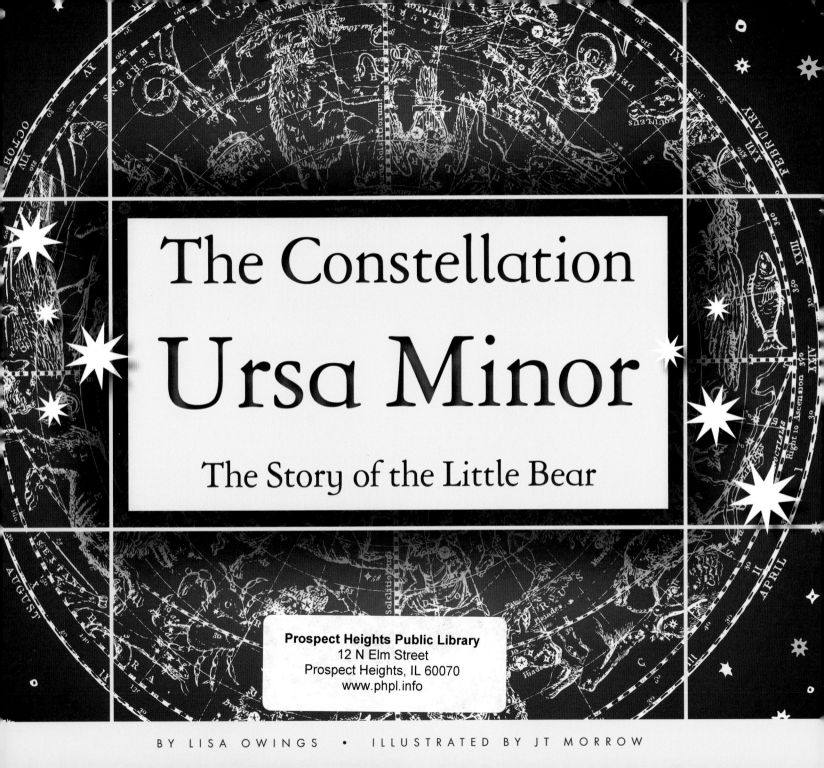

The Constellation
Ursa Minor

The Story of the Little Bear

BY LISA OWINGS • ILLUSTRATED BY JT MORROW

Published by The Child's World®
1980 Lookout Drive • Mankato, MN 56003-1705
800-599-READ • www.childsworld.com

Acknowledgments
The Child's World®: Mary Berendes, Publishing Director
Red Line Editorial: Editorial direction and production
The Design Lab: Design

Photographs ©: amana images inc./Alamy, 4; Markus Gann/
Shutterstock Images, 5; NASA/SDO/Steele Hill, 6; Antonio Abrignani/
Shutterstock Images, 7; NASA/ESA/G. Bacon (STScl), 8; John A Davis/
Shutterstock Images, 9; Nebojsa S/Shutterstock Images, 11; Panos
Karas/Shutterstock Images, 13; Harvard Map Collection, 15; John
Copland/Shutterstock Images, 17; Redsapphire/Shutterstock Images,
26; Universal Images Group/Getty Images, 27

Design elements: Alisafoytik/Dreamstime

ISBN: 9781623234904
LCCN: 2013931379

Printed in the United States of America
Mankato, MN
July, 2013
PA02168

ABOUT THE AUTHOR

Lisa Owings has a degree in English and creative writing from the University of Minnesota. She has written and edited a wide variety of educational books for young people. Lisa lives in Andover, Minnesota, where she can see Ursa Minor every night.

ABOUT THE ILLUSTRATOR

JT Morrow has worked as a freelance illustrator for more than 20 years and has won several awards. He also works in graphic design and animation. Morrow lives just south of San Francisco, California, with his wife and daughter.

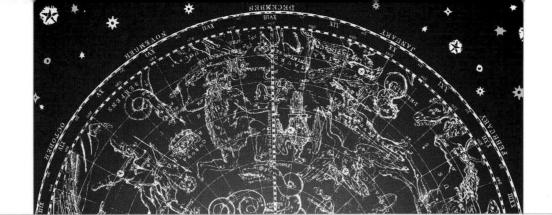

Table of Contents

CHAPTER 1

The Constellation Ursa Minor

People have long watched the movements of stars. The stars wheel across the sky. They rise and set each night. They move through the seasons of the year, too. As we watch the sky, Earth spins. We don't feel as though we are moving. But we are carried with it all the same. That is why the Sun seems to rise and set. It is why the stars seem to circle the heavens. For centuries, one star has held a special place in the northern sky. It shines almost directly above the North Pole, the center of the spinning top of Earth.

▲ The Little Bear's myth explains why its tail is so long.

▶ Opposite page: As Earth turns, the stars seem to wheel around a central point: the star Polaris.

Because of this, it never seems to move. This star is called Polaris, or the North Star.

Polaris and the stars around it form the constellation Ursa Minor, the Little Bear. The ancient Greeks told stories about this group of stars. One story said the Little Bear was once the goddess Ida. She cared for the infant god Zeus when he was in danger. Zeus later became the ruler of all the gods. He remembered how Ida took care of him. He wanted to honor her. So he set her among the stars in the shape of a Little Bear.

What Are Stars?

It is easy to think of stars as tiny lights. But really they are giant, fiery balls of churning, burning gas. They can burn for billions of years. The closest star to Earth is the Sun. Even at 93 million miles (150 million km) away, its light dazzles the eyes. Its heat prickles the skin. There are billions of stars in the night sky. Many are hundreds of times bigger and brighter than the Sun. And most are trillions of miles farther away.

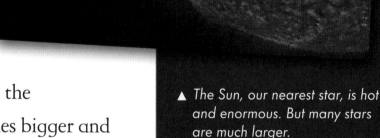

▲ The Sun, our nearest star, is hot and enormous. But many stars are much larger.

Patterns in the Sky

We can see only a small fraction of the stars from Earth. They decorate the night sky in bright patterns. For ancient stargazers, some groups

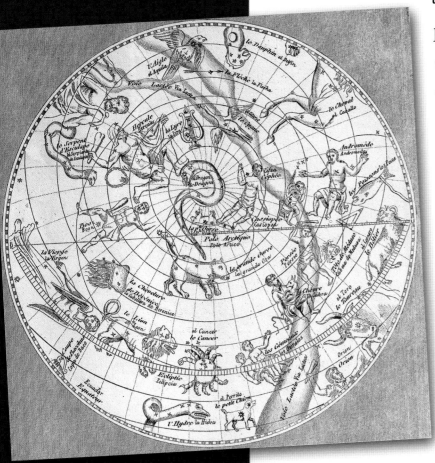

of stars stood out more than others. Their stars were very bright. Or they formed familiar shapes. Since long ago, people have traced pictures in these stars. They told stories about the pictures. These groups of stars are called constellations. Today there are 88 constellations. The Greek **astronomer** Ptolemy wrote down the first 48 almost 2,000 years ago. Forty more were added later. The entire sky is split into these 88 divisions. Each star in the night sky belongs to one of the constellations.

The North Star

Polaris is the most important star in Ursa Minor. It lights the tip of the Little Bear's tail. For centuries, it has been the closest star to the North Pole. It serves as a bright **compass** in northern skies. Countless sailors have relied on it to keep their ships on course.

There was slavery in the United States before the Civil War (1861–1865). Slaves in the South escaped to the North where slavery was illegal. Polaris led them northward to freedom.

Polaris has not always held its unique position. Like a top, Earth wobbles as it spins. It wobbles very, very slowly. So the North Pole doesn't always point to the same star. Since long ago, the North Pole has been tipping toward Polaris. Someday Earth will slowly wobble away again. Then a new star will take Polaris's place above the pole.

Polaris is not alone at the top of the world. It is part of a system of three stars. One of its smaller companions is relatively easy to spot. The other is so close to Polaris that it is almost impossible to see. Only the **Hubble Space Telescope** shows the two as separate stars.

Polaris B

Polaris Ab

Polaris A

▲ *The three stars of Polaris*

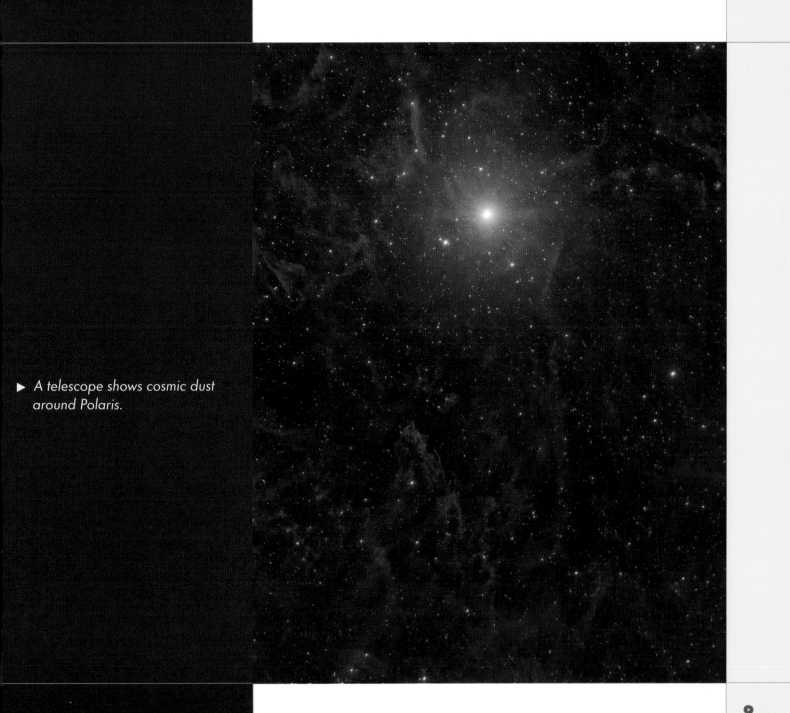

► A telescope shows cosmic dust around Polaris.

Other Stars in Ursa Minor: The Little Dipper

The seven brightest stars of Ursa Minor form a familiar pattern. They look like the Big Dipper in Ursa Major. But this group of stars is smaller. It is known as the Little Dipper. The handle of the Little Dipper is also the long tail of the Little Bear. It has three stars. Polaris is the brightest. The star below Polaris is Yildun. Epsilon Ursae Minoris is the third star in the handle.

The Little Dipper's bowl has four stars. The two closest to the handle are Zeta Ursae Minoris and Eta Ursae Minoris. These stars are faint compared to Pherkad and Kochab. Pherkad shines at the bottom

GUARDIANS OF THE POLE
The stars Pherkad and Kochab are called the Guardians of the Pole. They spend their nights marching around Polaris, seeming to keep watch. Ancient Arabs had another name for these two stars. They called them the Two Calves. The calves kept close to their mother, Polaris.

corner of the dipper's bowl. Kochab is brighter still—almost as bright as Polaris. It marks the rim of the bowl, where water might pour out. The stars of the dipper's bowl outline the body of the Little Bear.

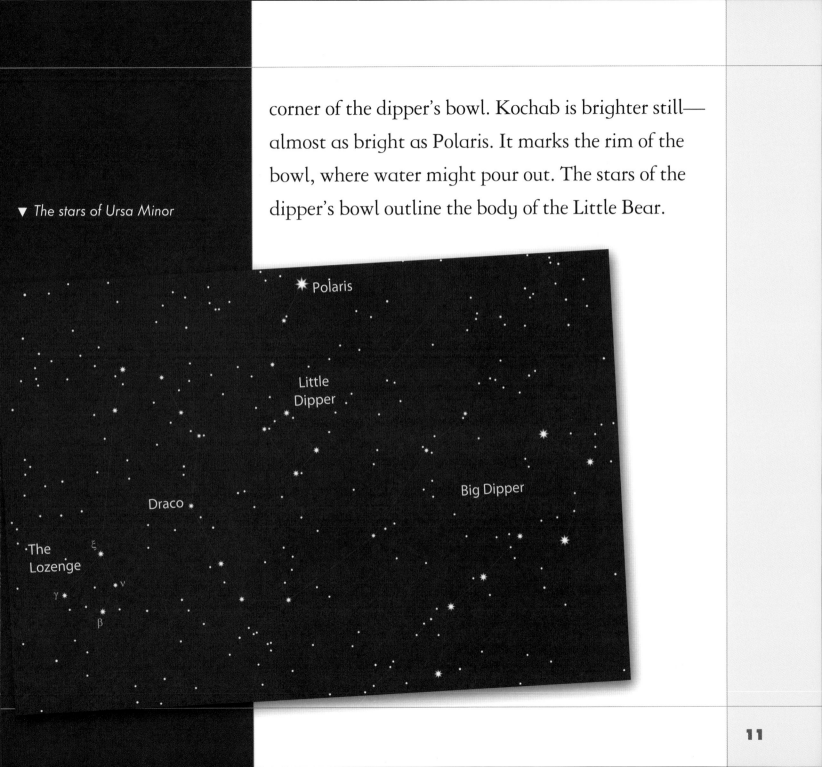

CHAPTER 2

The Origin of the Myth of Ursa Minor

Thousands of years ago, the Phoenicians sailed gleaming wooden ships over the Mediterranean Sea. The sailors were skilled at finding their way on ocean waters. They used the stars of Ursa Minor to guide them. They knew the stars showed them the way north.

The wise astronomer Thales was likely born in Phoenicia. He knew of the constellation that guided Phoenician sailors. Later, he moved to Greece. Greek sailors used a different set of stars. They used the

▲ *This modern replica shows what ancient Greek boats looked like.*

constellation Ursa Major, the Great Bear. Stories say Thales taught the Greeks about Ursa Minor around 600 BC. He suggested that sailors steer by this smaller group of stars.

The Phoenicians and the Greeks spent a lot of time at sea. If they did not know which stars to steer by, their ships would be lost. Greek sailors had good reason to rely on Ursa Major. Her stars were bright and easy to see as night fell. But after Thales taught them about Ursa Minor, the sailors saw her stars were better guides. They were harder to see. But they moved in a tighter circle around the northern pole. That meant they were a more exact compass. To this day, Ursa Minor and the star Polaris are known as the markers of true north.

From Dragon's Wings to Little Bear

Ursa Minor is nestled close to another constellation. The **coils** of the star-dragon Draco surround the Little Bear. It is said that long ago, the stars of Ursa Minor were seen as Draco's wings. But Thales noticed—or he knew from the Phoenicians—that these stars looked like a smaller Ursa Major. So he described a separate constellation instead of the dragon's wings. It became known as the Little Bear.

The ancient Greeks welcomed this new constellation. By around 300 BC, they fit it into their stories about Ursa Major. The Greek poet Aratus said the two bears in the sky were from the island of Crete. They had cared for the god Zeus when he was an infant. Many versions of this story are told today.

▶ *Opposite page: Draco lost its wings when Ursa Minor was created.*

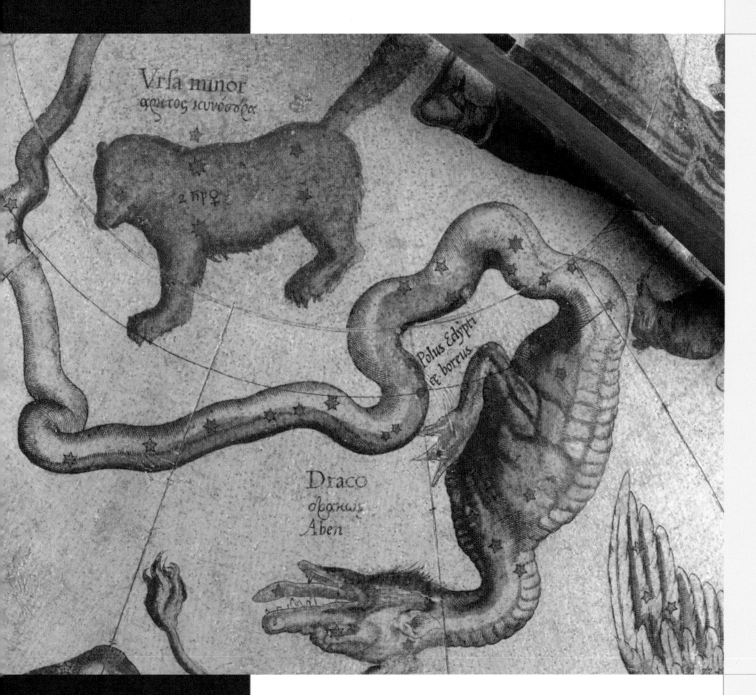

Zeus's Birthplace

The myth of Ursa Minor was as important to the Greeks as her guiding stars. The story tells of the birth of Zeus. He was king among Greek gods. The ancient Greeks loved and **worshipped** Zeus. They wanted to feel connected to him. So when they told stories about his life, they often claimed to have been part of it. When Greeks told the story of Ursa Minor, they changed the place where Zeus was born. Cretans claimed he had been born on Crete. Arcadians said he had been born in Arcadia. Many Greeks claimed he had been born near where they lived. They changed other details, too. That is why there are so many versions of this story.

The Other Myth of Ursa Minor

Some Greeks told a very different story about Ursa Minor. They spoke of the love Zeus had for the beautiful huntress Callisto. The two had a son together named Arcas. This drove Zeus's wife crazy with jealousy. She punished Callisto by turning her into a bear. But Zeus still loved Callisto. And he loved his son. Zeus turned Arcas into a bear so he could recognize his mother. Then he set them both in the stars as the Great and Little Bears.

▼ Worship of Zeus was widespread in the ancient world. This temple to Zeus is in Cyrene in modern-day Libya.

CHAPTER 3

The Story of Ursa Minor

In the earliest days of the world, Mother Earth and Father Sky had many children. These powerful gods and goddesses were called Titans. The youngest, Cronus, became their king. His wife was Rhea. Soon they were expecting a child.

Mother Earth and Father Sky had seen the future. They warned Cronus that one of his children would someday take his place as king. The mighty Cronus was filled with fear. He could not let someone else become king. So he hatched a terrible plan.

As soon as Rhea gave birth, Cronus tore the infant from her arms. He opened his mouth wide.

Then he swallowed the newborn child. Rhea's eyes went round with horror. She could not believe what her husband had done. Her heart broke for her lost child. Rhea had more children. But her husband swallowed every single one.

After Cronus had **devoured** five of her children, Rhea became pregnant again. She could not bear to lose another child. But she did not know how to stop Cronus. She begged Mother Earth and Father Sky to help her. They immediately took Rhea's side. They told her exactly what to do.

Rhea followed their advice. When it came time for her to give birth, she went to the island of Crete. There she secretly brought her son into the world. She called him Zeus. Mother Earth took the child in her vast arms. She hid him in a dark mountain cave. Two goddesses, Ida and Adrasteia, lived nearby. They agreed to care for the young god.

Rhea was glad her son was safe. Now she had to fool her husband. She found a heavy stone. Around it she wrapped a soft blanket. She cradled the stone in her arms and took it to her husband. As Rhea hoped, Cronus mistook the bundle for his son. He snatched up the stone and swallowed it whole.

Inside the cave on Crete, Ida and Adrasteia looked after Zeus. They fed him golden honey. A goat called Amaltheia offered him her milk. When it was time to sleep, they rocked Zeus in a golden cradle. Adrasteia made a pretty toy for him, a golden ball. Zeus loved to throw it in the air. A trail of light followed the ball wherever it went. **Warriors** stood guard outside the cave. They shouted and beat their shields with their spears. The noise kept Zeus's cries from reaching Cronus's ears.

Zeus grew up quickly on the island of Crete. He was furious when he learned what his father had done. But Mother Earth knew a way to get **revenge**. Zeus's mother helped him with the task. She made a special potion for Zeus to mix into his father's drink. Thirsty Cronus drank it all. Then he began to feel ill. Suddenly, he vomited up a heavy stone. Then one by one, he threw up each of Zeus's brothers and sisters.

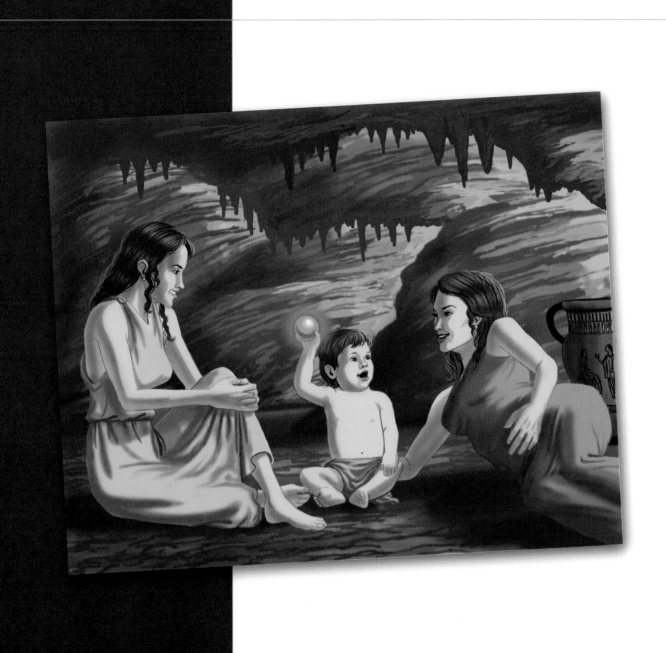

Zeus's siblings were happy to be free. They joined him in a battle against Cronus and the other Titans. After ten long years, Zeus and his followers won the war. They defeated the monstrous Cronus. Zeus became king of the gods, just as Mother Earth and Father Sky had said.

With a thunderbolt in hand, Zeus ruled the skies. But he never forgot the goddesses who were like mothers to him. Ida and Adrasteia had saved his life. Zeus wanted to honor them. Giving them the shapes of mighty bears, he swung them by their tails into the sky. That is why their tails are so long.

Adrasteia became the Great Bear. The Little Bear was Ida. No one quite knows why Zeus turned them into bears. Perhaps he was afraid they would get cold in northern skies. He knew fur coats would keep them warm so they could shine throughout the night.

CHAPTER 4

Ursa Minor in Other Cultures

The stars around the **celestial pole** have always seemed to rule the heavens. People often connected them with gods or kings. The ancient Egyptians linked Ursa Minor with their god Seth. Seth was a god of storms and confusion. The Chinese saw the palace of an **emperor**. Some say the Chinese called Polaris the "Great Emperor of Heaven." Many peoples, including Sumerians and

▼ Many cultures link the stars near Polaris with kings or gods.

Orion, the hunter

Taurus, the bull

Perseus

Gemini, the twins

Cancer, the crab

Auriga, the wagoner

Andromeda

Leo, the lion

Pole Star, the north star

Cassiopeia

Pegasus, the winged horse

Ursa Major, the great bear

Cepheus

Ursa Minor, the little bear

Hercules

Cygnus, the swan

Corona Borealis, the northern crown

Lyra, the lyre

Milky Way

Scandinavians, traced the shape of a mountain or hill in Ursa Minor's stars. They believed this was the home of the gods.

Many Europeans saw the constellation as a wagon or **chariot**. Others imagined it as a trumpet-shaped horn. Native Americans had their own stories about Ursa Minor. One story told of a mountain sheep who wanted to climb the highest peak. He climbed until he fell into a crack. He grew afraid. But the only way out was to keep climbing. Finally he came out at the top of the sky. His father saw him there and was very proud. He turned his son into a star so everyone could see him. That is how the mountain sheep became the star Polaris.

CHAPTER 5

How to Find Ursa Minor

Ursa Minor is a small, faint constellation. The best way to find it is to look for Polaris. You can use the Big Dipper as a guide. Find the two stars of the dipper's bowl that are farthest from the handle. These stars are called the "Pointers." Draw an imaginary line from the star at the bottom of the bowl through the one at the top. The next bright star the line crosses will be Polaris.

Once you've found the tip of the Little Bear's tail, look for the two bright Guardians of the Pole. If it is clear enough, the dimmer stars between the Guardians and Polaris will come into view.

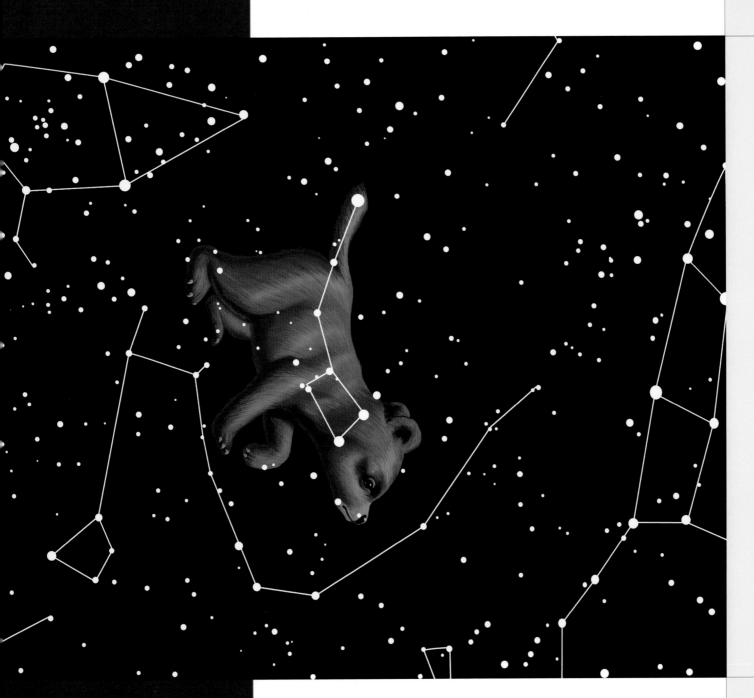

Glossary

astronomer (uh-STRAW-nuh-mur)
A scientist who studies stars and other objects in space is called an astronomer. The astronomer discovered a new star.

celestial pole (suh-LES-chul POHL)
The celestial pole is the place in the night sky that stays still. The constellations seem to wheel around the celestial pole.

chariot (CHAR-ee-uht)
A chariot is a small vehicle pulled by horses. Ursa Minor is like a chariot being driven around the sky.

coils (COYLZ)
Coils are loops or spirals. The body of Draco has coils.

compass (KUM-puhs)
A compass is a tool that always points north. A sailor uses a compass to find her way.

devoured (di-VOWRD)
If something is devoured, it is hungrily eaten. Cronus devoured his children.

emperor (EHM-puh-ruhr)
An emperor is a male ruler. Polaris is like an emperor in the sky.

Hubble Space Telescope (HUB-uhl SPAYS TEHL-uh-skohp)
The Hubble Space Telescope is a large telescope in space. The Hubble Space Telescope takes detailed pictures of space objects.

revenge (ruh-VEHNJ)
Revenge is getting someone back for something bad they did. Zeus and Rhea took revenge on Cronus.

warriors (WAH-ree-uhrz)
Warriors are soldiers. Warriors made noise to protect Zeus.

worshipped (WUR-shipt)
If something is worshipped, it is loved and respected as a god. The ancient Greeks worshipped Zeus.

Learn More

Books

Dickinson, Rachel. *Tools of Navigation: A Kid's Guide to the History and Science of Finding Your Way.* White River Junction, VT: Nomad, 2005.

Napoli, Donna Jo. *Treasury of Greek Mythology: Classic Stories of Gods, Goddesses, Heroes, and Monsters.* Washington, DC: National Geographic Society, 2011.

Rey, H. A. *Find the Constellations.* 2nd ed. Boston: Houghton Mifflin, 2008.

Sparrow, Giles. *Night Sky.* New York: Scholastic, 2013.

Taylor, Carrie J. *All the Stars in the Sky: Native Stories from the Heavens.* Toronto: Tundra Books, 2006.

Web Sites

Visit our Web site for links about Ursa Minor:

childsworld.com/links

Note to Parents, Teachers, and Librarians:
We routinely verify our Web links to make sure they are safe and active sites. So encourage your readers to check them out!

Index